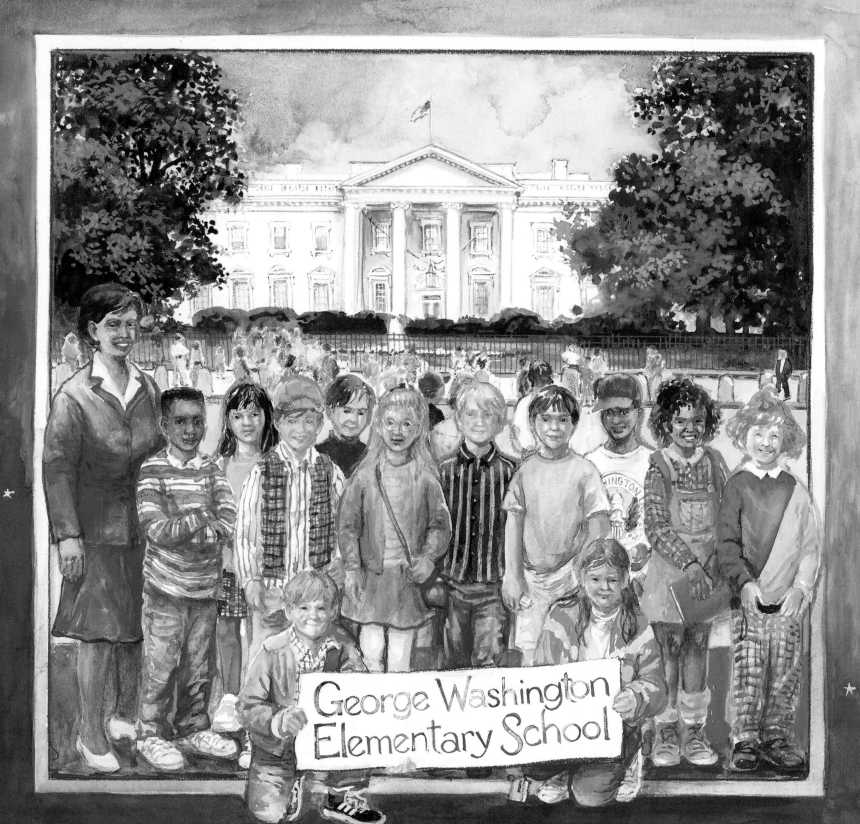

GHOSTS

of the

WHITE HOUSE

By Cheryl Harness

Aladdin Paperbacks
New York London Toronto Sydney Singapore

Acknowledgments

I wish to thank and acknowledge the office of the Curator of the White House and the staff of the Harry S. Truman Presidential Library, Independence, Missouri. I also thank former president Gerald R. Ford for his kind assistance.

First Aladdin Paperbacks edition January 2002
Copyright © 1998 by Cheryl Harness

Aladdin Paperbacks
An imprint of Simon & Schuster
Children's Publishing Division
1230 Avenue of the Americas
New York, NY 10020

Also available in a Simon & Schuster Books for Young Readers hardcover edition.
The text of this book is set in 11-point Adobe Garamond semibold and 15-point One Stroke Script.
The illustrations are rendered in watercolor and color pencil.
Manufactured in China
4 6 8 10 9 7 5

The Library of Congress has cataloged the hardcover edition as follows:
Harness, Cheryl.
Ghosts of the White House / Cheryl Harness
p.———cm.
Includes bibliographical references.
Summary: George Washington's ghost pulls a girl out of her school White House tour and takes her on a personal tour of the building,
introducing her to the ghosts of previous presidents and to the history of the White House and of the United States.
ISBN: 0-689-80872-0 (hc.)
1. White House (Washington, D.C.)—Miscellanea—Juvenile literature. 2. Presidents—United States—Miscellanea—Juvenile literature. 3. Unites States—History—
Miscellanea—Juvenile literature. [1. White House (Washington, D.C.)—Miscellanea. 2. Presidents—Miscellanea. 3. United States—History—Miscellanea.] I. Title
F204.WfH37 1998
973'.09'9-dc21
96-39752 CIP AC
ISBN-10: 0-689-84892-7 (Aladdin pbk.)
ISBN-13: 978-0-689-84892-6 (Aladdin pbk.)

". . . big enough for two emperors, one Pope, and the Grand Lama."
—THOMAS JEFFERSON

"It really is a little house."
—PRINCE CHARLES
of ENGLAND

THE WHITE HOUSE

"If you are as happy, my dear sir, on entering this house as I am in leaving it and returning home, you are the happiest man in the country."
—JAMES BUCHANAN to ABRAHAM LINCOLN
March 4, 1861

"I pray Heaven to bestow the best of blessings on this house, and on all that shall hereafter inhabit it. May none but honest and wise men ever rule under this roof."
—JOHN ADAMS

"This House is built for ages to come."
—ABIGAIL ADAMS

"It's the best public housing I've ever seen."
—GERALD R. FORD

"I consider history—our history—to be a source of strength to us here in the White House and to all the American people. Anything which dramatizes the great story of the United States—as I think the White House does—is worthy of the closest attention and respect by Americans who live here and who visit here and who are part of our citizenry."
—JOHN F. KENNEDY

★ 1600 Pennsylvania Avenue · Washington, D.C.

I wish I were a president's kid. I'd be famous AND I'd get to live in the White House. It's so OLD—I bet it could even be HAUNTED. Late at night, I'd explore for hidden passageways. It'd be so cool! Imagine: Living in the same big, old house where all those presidents and all of their families have lived for almost TWO HUNDRED YEARS...

I'll bet Abraham Lincoln looked out this very window, thinking about how to run the whole country!

Time for dinner, Sara.

Coming, Mr. President— I mean, Dad!

The GROUND FLOOR

Library

kitchen

Ground Floor Corridor

Map Room

Diplomatic Reception Room

China Room

Vermeil Room

There are two basements down below.

So, when I found out that my class was going on a field trip to the White House, I was really excited. We'd have to write a report, of course, when we got back. And before we went, we had to look up lots of facts about it, so we wouldn't be stupid on the tour. I even found out how the rooms go.

Maybe I'd get to see the real-life PRESIDENT OF THE UNITED STATES OF AMERICA! Anyway, I'd get to see his house—IN PERSON.

The WHITE HOUSE

was designed by an Irish architect named James Hoban. The building was begun on Saturday, October 13, 1792. Fire, in 1814, then old age, in 1949, caused it to be twice rebuilt. The House is about 70 feet tall, 168 feet wide, east to west, and 85 feet wide, north to south.

The FIRST FLOOR

The North Portico was added in 1829.

West Wing

Family Dining Room

Entrance Hall

State Dining Room

Red Room

Blue Room

Green Room

Cross Hall

East Room

The South Portico was built in 1824.

The SECOND FLOOR

West Sitting Hall

Center Hall

Queen's Bedroom

East Sitting Hall

Yellow Oval Room

The President's Office (Treaty Room)

The Lincoln Bedroom

Lincoln Sitting Room

This balcony was President Truman's idea in 1948.

There are more rooms upstairs on the third floor.

East Wing

There are 132 rooms, some public, some not, in the main building. Mostly offices, including the Oval Office, are in the Wings.

WILLIAM HENRY HARRISON

Feb. 9, 1773–Apr. 4, 1841
"Old Tippecanoe"
9TH PRESIDENT
MAR.-APRIL 1841

Both Harrison and Tyler were soldiers in the Indian Wars and the War of 1812. Captain Harrison earned his nickname fighting Shawnee warrior Tecumseh on the Tippecanoe River in the Indiana Territory in 1811. Exactly one month after his inauguration, W. H. Harrison became the first president to die in office.

JAMES GARFIELD

Nov. 19, 1831–Sept. 19, 1881
"Canal Boy"
20TH PRESIDENT MAR.–SEPT. 1881

He was born in an Ohio log cabin and became a deckhand on a canal boat, then a professor of Latin and Greek, and then a lawyer, Civil War hero, and congressman. Only four months after taking office, James Garfield became the second president to be assassinated: He was shot by Charles Guiteau, who was mad about not getting a government job.

ZACHARY TAYLOR

Nov. 24, 1784–July 9, 1850
"Old Rough-and-Ready"
12TH PRESIDENT 1849–50

Zachary Taylor became a hero in President Polk's war with Mexico. Taylor's term of office was in the Gold Rush days, when slavery and California statehood were the hot issues.

Mr. Harrison was the first president to die in office. There was a big political argument then: Would Mr. Tyler be a stand-in until a new president was elected? Or would he, as vice president, automatically become president?

There were folks who tried to throw me out, but the office was MINE, by golly! And that's how it's been ever since: when a president dies, the vice president becomes next in line.

JOHN TYLER

Mar. 29, 1790–Jan. 18, 1862
"Accidental President"
10TH PRESIDENT 1841–45

"Tippecanoe and Tyler Too": This was the slogan that got voters to the polls in 1840. They wanted W. H. Harrison, the Indian War Soldier. Instead, the voters got his vice president. John Tyler, the first president to get married while he was in office, had so many political enemies that he was known as the president without a party.

JAMES MADISON

Mar. 16, 1751–June 28, 1836
"Father of the Constitution"
4TH PRESIDENT 1809–17

Because British ships were attacking U.S. ships on the high seas and some congressmen still wanted to try to capture Canada from England, President Madison declared war, the War of 1812. President Madison and his wife, Dolley, had to flee the White House just before invading British soldiers set it on fire. Mr. Madison was five feet four inches tall, the shortest president. Mr. Lincoln was a foot taller, the tallest president.

JAMES MONROE

Apr. 28, 1758–July 4, 1831
"Last of the Cocked Hats"
5TH PRESIDENT 1817–25

President Madison's secretary of state was the last of the Revolutionary leaders to become president. James Monroe's time is sometimes called "the era of good feeling." We were getting along better with England and had settled with Spain over Florida. Americans gathered their optimism and know-how and built the Erie Canal. Most important, President Monroe declared that European meddling in the Americas was wanted no longer. That was the Monroe Doctrine.

I'm pleased to introduce Mr. Madison, one of the chief inventors of our government. He helped write the U.S. Constitution in 1787.

It is not enough to win a revolution, Miss Sara. Making a nation that will last —that's the noble victory!

I am honored to meet a young American who may live to celebrate the three hundredth year of our republic in 2076.

In your lifetime, may you see our country living wisely with the nations of the world.

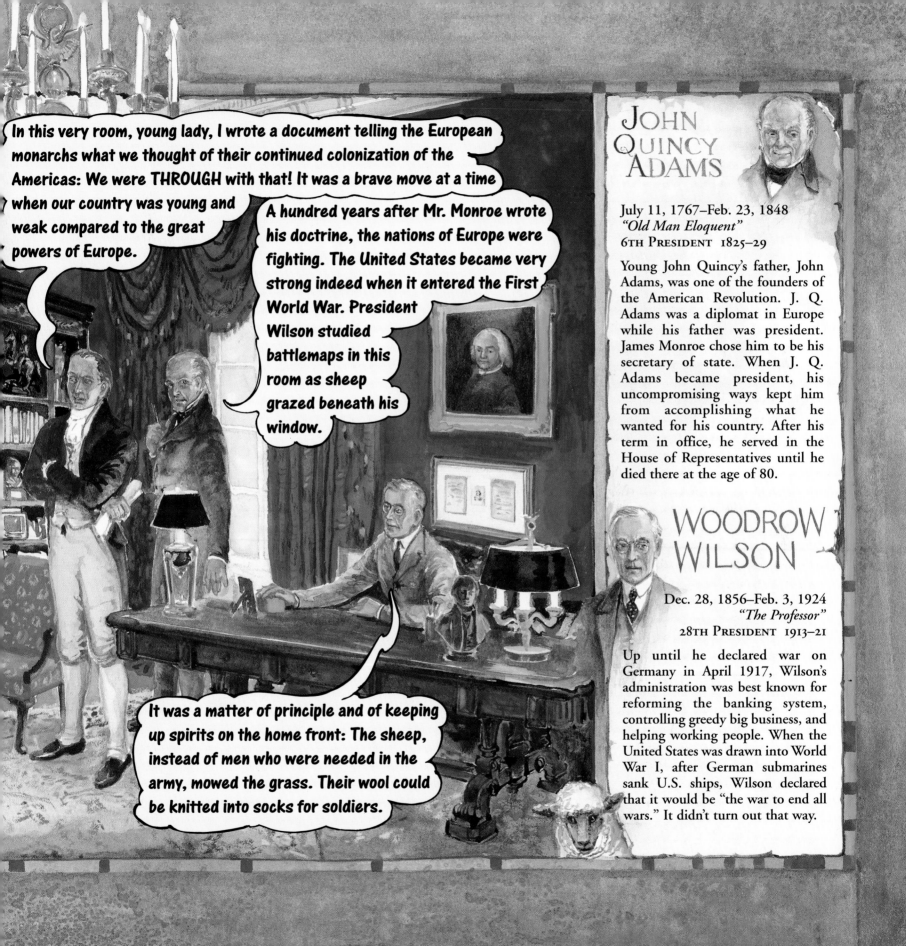

In this very room, young lady, I wrote a document telling the European monarchs what we thought of their continued colonization of the Americas: We were THROUGH with that! It was a brave move at a time when our country was young and weak compared to the great powers of Europe.

A hundred years after Mr. Monroe wrote his doctrine, the nations of Europe were fighting. The United States became very strong indeed when it entered the First World War. President Wilson studied battlemaps in this room as sheep grazed beneath his window.

It was a matter of principle and of keeping up spirits on the home front: The sheep, instead of men who were needed in the army, mowed the grass. Their wool could be knitted into socks for soldiers.

JOHN QUINCY ADAMS

July 11, 1767–Feb. 23, 1848
"Old Man Eloquent"
6TH PRESIDENT 1825–29

Young John Quincy's father, John Adams, was one of the founders of the American Revolution. J. Q. Adams was a diplomat in Europe while his father was president. James Monroe chose him to be his secretary of state. When J. Q. Adams became president, his uncompromising ways kept him from accomplishing what he wanted for his country. After his term in office, he served in the House of Representatives until he died there at the age of 80.

WOODROW WILSON

Dec. 28, 1856–Feb. 3, 1924
"The Professor"
28TH PRESIDENT 1913–21

Up until he declared war on Germany in April 1917, Wilson's administration was best known for reforming the banking system, controlling greedy big business, and helping working people. When the United States was drawn into World War I, after German submarines sank U.S. ships, Wilson declared that it would be "the war to end all wars." It didn't turn out that way.

The Lincoln Bedroom

ABRAHAM LINCOLN

Feb. 12, 1809–Apr. 15, 1865
"Honest Abe the Railsplitter"
16TH PRESIDENT 1861–65

More than anything, the tall man from Springfield, Illinois, wanted to save the Union. The Civil War began over arguments about slavery, the rights of states and their citizens, and the power of the federal government in Washington. By the time the war was over, 600,000 American soldiers had been killed by other American soldiers and President Lincoln had written the Emancipation Proclamation (which led to freedom for four million slaves). "Uncle Abe, the Great Emancipator" saved the Union, then, less than a week after the war came to an end, he was shot by John Wilkes Booth.

"As I would not be a slave, so I would not be a master."

Oh, wow, Mr. Lincoln! It's so amazing to see you in person. Was this really your bedroom?

Well, no, little miss, it was my office. My wife Mary bought this big fancy bed for the spare bedroom. Our boy Willie died in it my second year in office...
Sara—my sister and my stepmother had that same pretty name. Well, Sara, I'm mighty glad the General plucked you out for the grand tour.

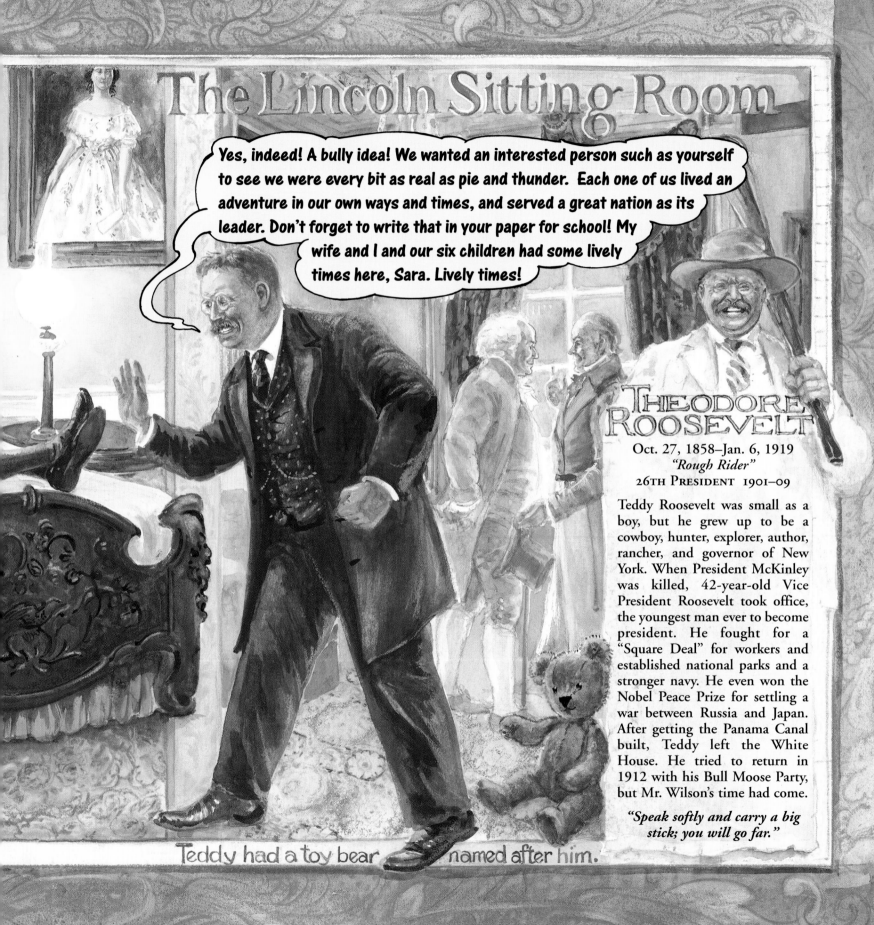

JAMES BUCHANAN

Apr. 23, 1791–June 1, 1868
"Old Buck"
15TH PRESIDENT 1857–61

The only bachelor president was a coolheaded statesman, but he couldn't stop the fury over slavery. He believed that slavery was wrong but that government hadn't the power to stop its spreading into Western lands, or to stop the Southern states from leaving the Union. President Buchanan was relieved to hand this hot potato to his successor, Mr. Lincoln of Illinois.

HERBERT HOOVER

Aug. 10, 1874–Oct. 20, 1964
"Chief"
31ST PRESIDENT 1929–33

He was a rich mining engineer who, during the First World War, organized a campaign to get food to people behind enemy lines. How could a brilliant, big-hearted hero like Herbert Hoover seem so helpless? Good times boomed in the 1920s, then went bust. No one knew exactly why. The banks began closing, and people lost their jobs and homes. They blamed the president, who seemed gloomy and uncertain.

Lyndon B. Johnson

Aug. 27, 1908–Jan. 22, 1973
"LBJ"
36TH PRESIDENT 1963–69

In the House and in the Senate, Lyndon Johnson of Texas became the master of getting his way with other politicians. When John Kennedy was killed, President Johnson launched a "War on Poverty" and fought injustice and pollution with government programs. LBJ's goal was called "the Great Society." Then he got hopelessly tangled in the Vietnam War. The popular president lost his power to persuade the people to see his point of view.

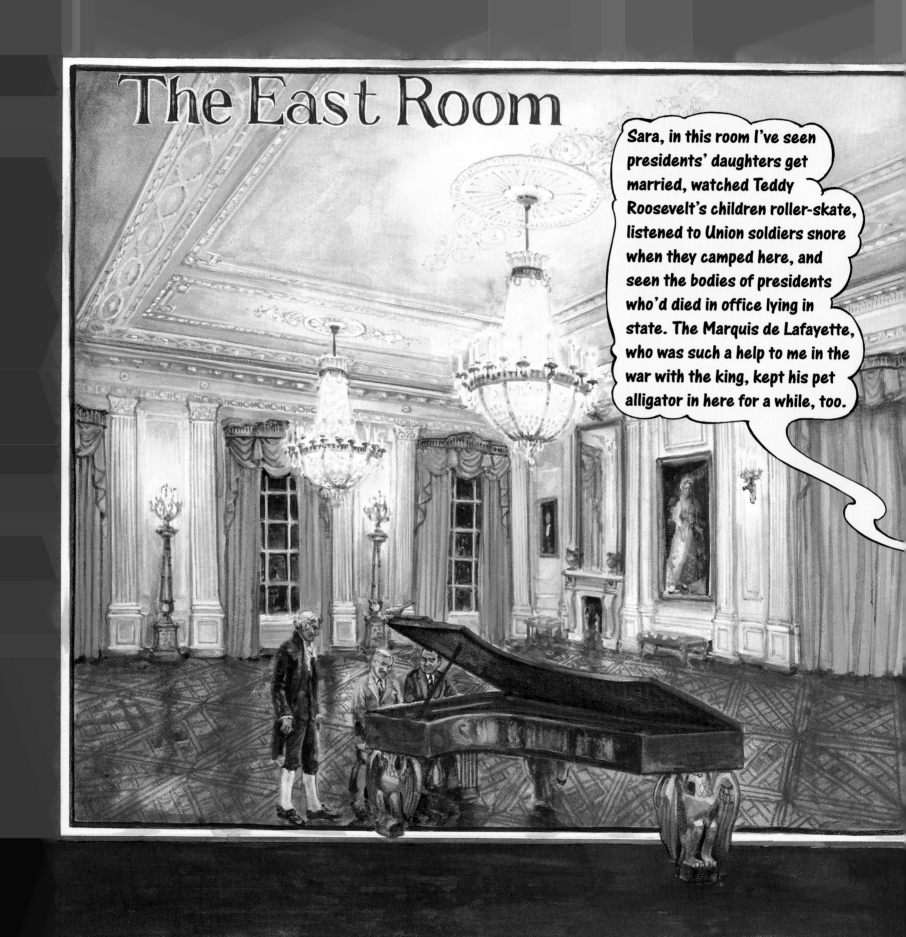

I hosted New Year's Day receptions and invited all citizens into the president's house. Not nearly as elegant as Mr. Arthur's concerts, but most democratic! People were packed in here! I can remember ladies in bonnets standing up on the chairs to get a good look at everybody, and folks snipping off bits of the curtains for souvenirs.

How rude!

Important documents have been signed and fancy receptions have been given in the East Room—and Mrs. John Adams hung her wet wash to dry in here, too! But, my dear young lady, I wish you could have seen the candles gleaming in the chandeliers and the ladies' diamonds glittering, as music filled this room during the grand concerts I held....

ANDREW JACKSON

Mar. 15, 1767–June 8, 1845
"Old Hickory"
7TH PRESIDENT 1829–37

Many folks in the growing frontier nation saw Andy Jackson as a hero because he had beaten the British in the Battle of New Orleans in the War of 1812. He defeated the more conservative John Quincy Adams in the hard-fought campaign of 1828. President Jackson stretched the power of his office by challenging and vetoing laws made by Congress.

CHESTER ARTHUR

Oct. 5, 1829–Nov. 18, 1886
"The Gentleman Boss"
21ST PRESIDENT 1881–85

President Garfield had wanted to make government civil service more honest, but he was assassinated. Vice President Arthur would be in charge now. His were the days of political "bosses" who gave out jobs and money to people who "voted right." People were surprised when "the Gentleman Boss" turned the tables and became a reformer. President Arthur modernized the U.S. Navy and the U.S. Post Office, too.

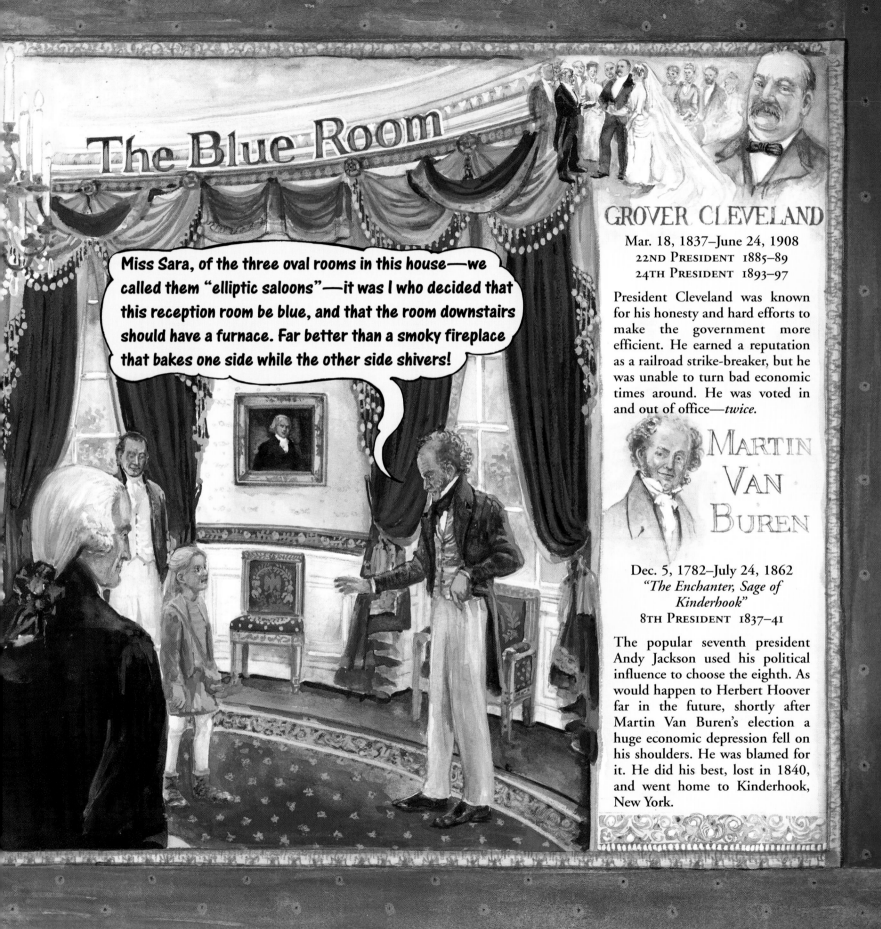

Warren G. Harding

Nov. 2, 1865–Aug. 2, 1923
29TH PRESIDENT 1921–23

Senator Harding of Ohio was handsome, kind, and unwilling to be president. He voted the way the Republican big shots told him to, and he got jobs for his buddies back home. As president, he trusted friends who tried to make money off the government. President Harding died, most likely of a heart attack, just as the lid was popping off a teapot full of scandals.

CALVIN COOLIDGE

July 4, 1872–Jan. 5, 1933
"Silent Cal"
30TH PRESIDENT 1923–29

After President Harding died, ending his crooked administration, his vice president, a sour-faced New Englander, entered the White House. People liked his quiet, honest ways. Business was booming, so "Silent Cal" just left things alone and kept his mouth shut.

"The business of America is business."

The Green Room

Did you know that this used to be Mr. Jefferson's dining room, Mr. Coolidge? The Monroes used this for a card room; I wonder if there is a deck of cards around here. Say, Calvin, look at this portrait of Benjamin Franklin. He looks different with a wig, doesn't he? Calvin? Mr. Coolidge? Say, I have a bet with Mr. Truman that I can get you to say three entire words today.

You lose.

The Red Room

Up until two days before I took the oath of office, here in this room, the country wasn't sure who the next president would be. The vote was so close and fierce that some boldly said that my Republican Party stole the election of 1876.

1876: the hundredth birthday of the nation. The poor country was still torn up and getting over the Civil War. Not until then—in President Hayes's term, twelve years after the war—did northern troops pull out of the South.

Franklin Pierce

Nov. 23, 1804–Oct. 8, 1869
"Handsome Frank"
14TH PRESIDENT 1853–57

"Abolish slavery forever!" "Keep slavery in the South and nowhere else!" "Let each state mind its own business!" "Let the people in the territories vote yes or no!" The voices were getting louder and angrier across the nation. President Pierce bowed to Southern interests and brought the Civil War a little closer.

Rutherford B. Hayes

Oct. 4, 1822–Jan. 17, 1893
"Dark Horse President"
19TH PRESIDENT 1877–81

Twelve years after the Civil War ended, President Hayes pulled federal troops out of Louisiana, officially ending the Reconstruction of the South. He was an honest man who inherited a corrupt system in which plenty of people had jobs in the government because politicians owed them favors, not because they could do the jobs well. President Hayes tried hard to make the government more fair.

"If a nation expects to be ignorant and free, it expects what never was and never will be."

Thomas Jefferson

Apr. 13, 1743–July 4, 1826
"Long Tom, Father of the Declaration of Independence"
3RD PRESIDENT 1801–09

Thomas Jefferson, the self-taught architect, believed that government should be in the hands of an educated people. This president was a naturalist who sent Lewis and Clark to explore the wonders of the Louisiana Purchase: 827,987 square miles of land that he bought from Napoleon. Then he sent the navy to fight the Barbary pirates off the coast of Africa. Thomas Jefferson suffered the "splendid misery" of the presidency, then returned to his home, Monticello.

Lewis and Clark had a hard eight-thousand-mile trek through the Louisiana Purchase, and on to the sea. In my day, the Queen of England claimed control of the Oregon Territory. I made it my business to fix THAT, and I meant to have California too! Our nation's manifest destiny was to stretch out to the Pacific Ocean.

James Knox Polk

Nov. 2, 1795–June 15, 1849
"Napoleon of the Stump"
11TH PRESIDENT 1845–49

Americans believed that the U.S. should go all the way to the Pacific Ocean, down to Mexico, and up to Canada. Polk wanted Texas and California in the Union even if it meant declaring war against Mexico, which the U.S. did, and then won the right to buy the southwestern lands. As for the Oregon Territory, a compromise with England established the present border with Canada in 1846.

ANDREW JOHNSON

Dec. 29, 1808–July 31, 1875
"The Tennessee Tailor"
17TH PRESIDENT 1865–69

Lincoln had been buried, the Civil War was over and the beaten South was ruined. What a sad mess President Johnson had before him! He wanted the Union back together quickly, but radical Republican congressmen wanted to punish the South. The argument led to the President's being impeached. While this was going on, Native Americans were fighting for their land and their ways of life in the West.

Benjamin Harrison

Aug. 20, 1833–Mar. 13, 1901
"Little Ben"
23RD PRESIDENT 1889–93

Like all the presidents since U.S. Grant, the grandson of W.H. Harrison wanted to reform civil service; but he, too, faced a lot of opposition from folks who liked things the way they were. President Harrison enlarged the navy and increased the taxes on goods imported from foreign countries.

The Library

Why, Mr. Johnson, they've cleaned the greasy, grimy basement! And the laundry room is full of books!

I'll bet there are still rats and mice skittering in the walls, though. My daughter, Martha, fought a war with them: setting sneaky cats, poison, and traps on the poor little fellows. But I set out flour and water for them up in my room. The mice had faith in me—that's more than I could say for the gents in Congress!

The China Room

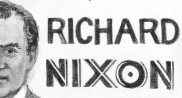

Millard Fillmore

Jan. 7, 1800–Mar. 8, 1874
13TH PRESIDENT 1850–53

"Old Rough-and-Ready" President Taylor was dead. Now Mr. Fillmore's time had come to smooth the angry feelings between the North and South over slavery. The Compromise of 1850, which called for tougher runaway slave laws but forbade slavery in California, put off the Civil War—but only for a while.

RICHARD NIXON

Jan. 9, 1913–Apr. 22, 1994
37TH PRESIDENT 1969–74

Once he had been Eisenhower's vice president, then he was defeated by Kennedy in 1960. At last, Richard Nixon won the presidency in 1968. He improved international relations and, slowly, painfully, ended the Vietnam War. President Nixon was reelected partly because those around him cheated, and then the president lied about it. This was known as the Watergate scandal. Mr. Nixon, to avoid being impeached, resigned his office, the only president ever to do so.

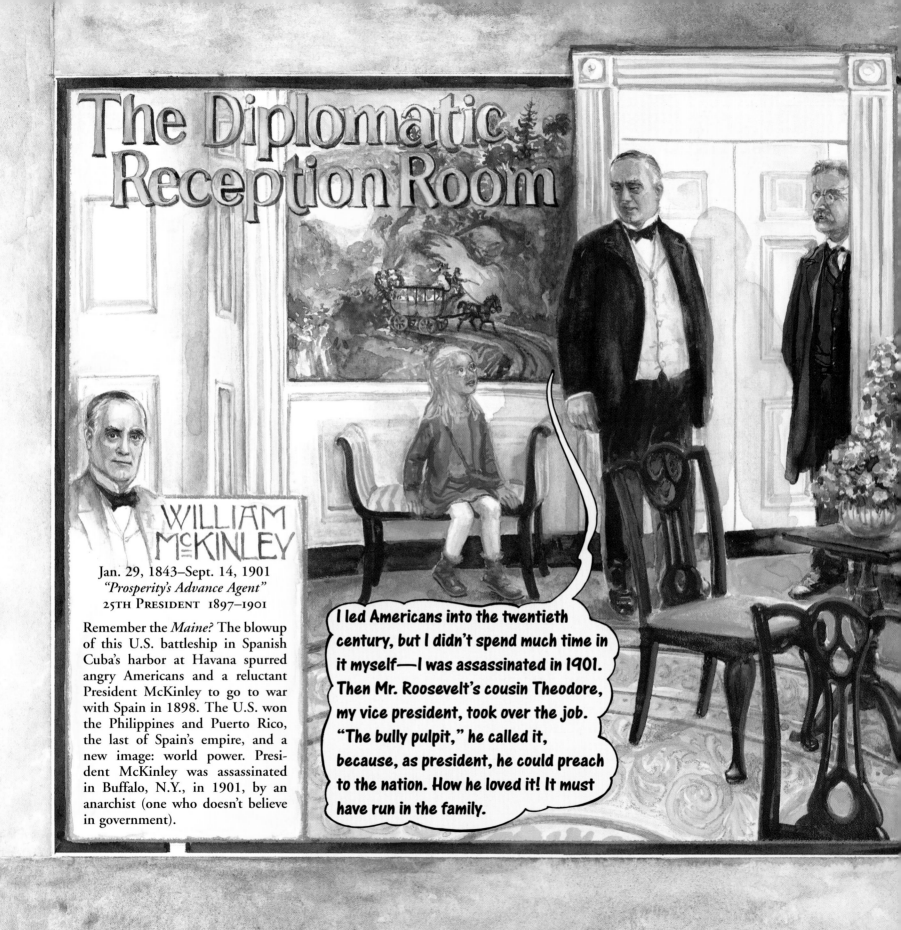

ULYSSES S. GRANT

Apr. 27, 1822–July 23,1885
*"Galena Tanner, the
Hero of Appomattox"*
18TH PRESIDENT 1869–77

He had failed at business and farming. But after the Civil War, this victorious Union general was a hero who became president. U.S. Grant was an honest man, but he trusted friends who mostly turned out to be crooks. His administration was dishonored. After leaving office, he was broke and sick. Mark Twain encouraged the old soldier to write a book about his life. U.S. Grant completed his autobiography, a best-seller, just before his death.

DWIGHT D. EISENHOWER

Oct. 14, 1890–Mar. 28, 1969
"Ike"
34TH PRESIDENT 1953–61

General Eisenhower was the commander of all the Allied Forces in Europe in World War II. As president, he ended the Korean War, begun during Truman's time. He sent U.S. soldiers to the capital of Arkansas to make sure that black students were allowed to go to school with white students. Ike was determined that civil rights laws be obeyed. When he was in the White House, the space race began. The Russians sent the first satellite, called *Sputnik,* into orbit around the earth.

The Map Room

The Oval Office

President Taft's pet cow, Pauline grazed on the White House lawn.

WILLIAM HOWARD TAFT

Sept. 15, 1857–Mar. 8, 1930
"Big Bill"
27TH PRESIDENT 1909–13

Mr. Taft wanted to be a judge on the Supreme Court, but Teddy Roosevelt and Mrs. Taft talked him into running for president. He won, then did his best fighting big business monopolies and working for the conservation of natural resources. In 1912, President Taft lost a three-way race to both Teddy Roosevelt *and* Woodrow Wilson, and was glad of it. At last, in 1921, "Big Bill" was appointed Chief Justice of the Supreme Court.

The biggest President ordered a special bathtub.

Four men could fit in it.

The President of the United States is the chief ● commander in chief of military forces ● chief of state

The White House became so crowded with visitors, workers, and the president's family that office space had to be added on. The West Wing, including the President's new Oval Office, was completed in 1909. President Taft was the first to use it, were you not?

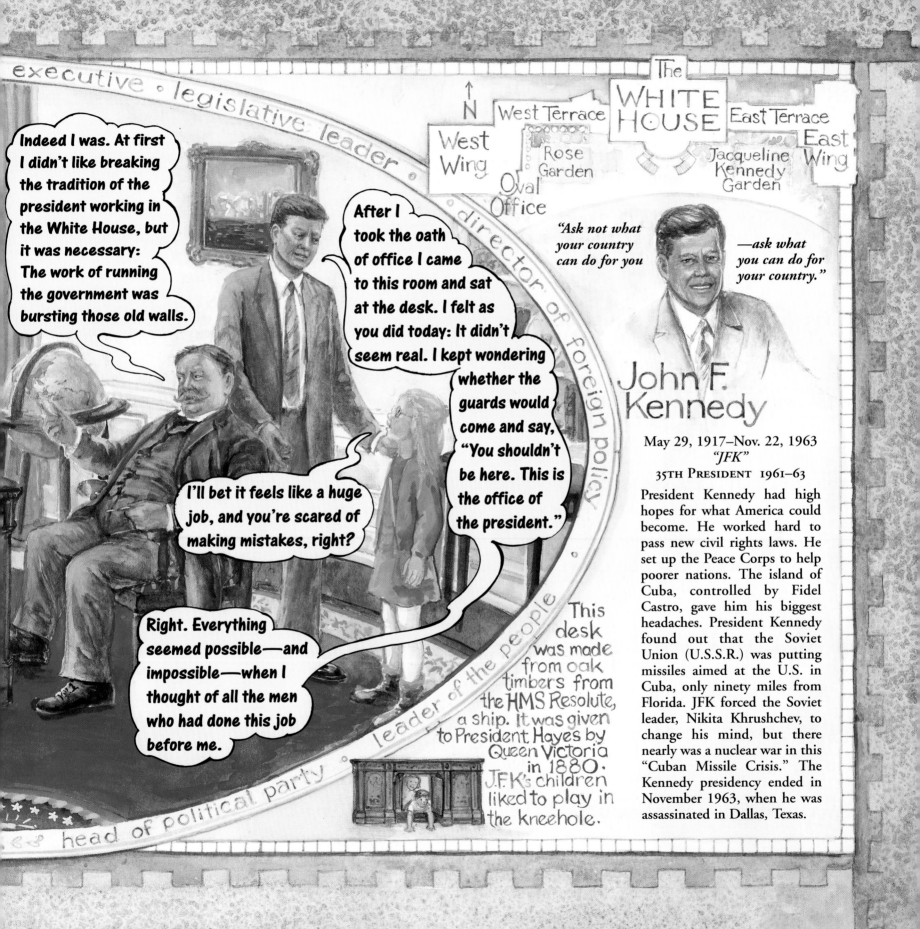

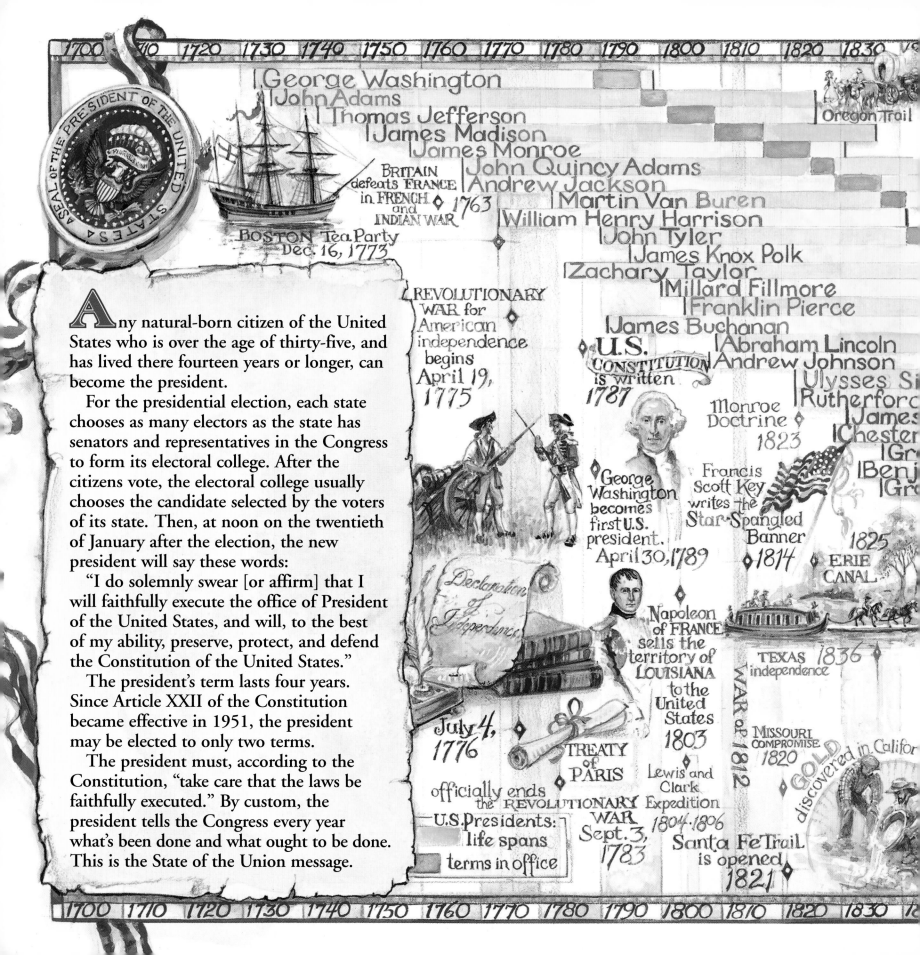

George Washington
John Adams
Thomas Jefferson
James Madison
James Monroe
John Quincy Adams
Andrew Jackson
Martin Van Buren
William Henry Harrison
John Tyler
James Knox Polk
Zachary Taylor
Millard Fillmore
Franklin Pierce
James Buchanan
Abraham Lincoln
Andrew Johnson
Ulysses S.
Rutherford
James
Chester
Gr
Benj
Gr

Oregon Trail

BRITAIN defeats FRANCE in FRENCH and INDIAN WAR ◊ 1763

BOSTON Tea Party Dec. 16, 1773

Any natural-born citizen of the United States who is over the age of thirty-five, and has lived there fourteen years or longer, can become the president.

For the presidential election, each state chooses as many electors as the state has senators and representatives in the Congress to form its electoral college. After the citizens vote, the electoral college usually chooses the candidate selected by the voters of its state. Then, at noon on the twentieth of January after the election, the new president will say these words:

"I do solemnly swear [or affirm] that I will faithfully execute the office of President of the United States, and will, to the best of my ability, preserve, protect, and defend the Constitution of the United States."

The president's term lasts four years. Since Article XXII of the Constitution became effective in 1951, the president may be elected to only two terms.

The president must, according to the Constitution, "take care that the laws be faithfully executed." By custom, the president tells the Congress every year what's been done and what ought to be done. This is the State of the Union message.

REVOLUTIONARY WAR for American independence begins April 19, 1775

U.S. CONSTITUTION is written 1787

Monroe Doctrine ◊ 1823

George Washington becomes first U.S. president. April 30, 1789

Francis Scott Key writes the Star-Spangled Banner ◊ 1814

1825 ERIE CANAL

Declaration of Independence

Napoleon of FRANCE sells the territory of LOUISIANA to the United States 1803

TEXAS 1836 independence

July 4, 1776

TREATY of PARIS officially ends the REVOLUTIONARY WAR Sept. 3, 1783

Lewis and Clark Expedition 1804-1806

WAR of 1812

MISSOURI COMPROMISE 1820

GOLD discovered in Califor

U.S. Presidents: life spans terms in office

Santa Fe Trail is opened ◊ 1821

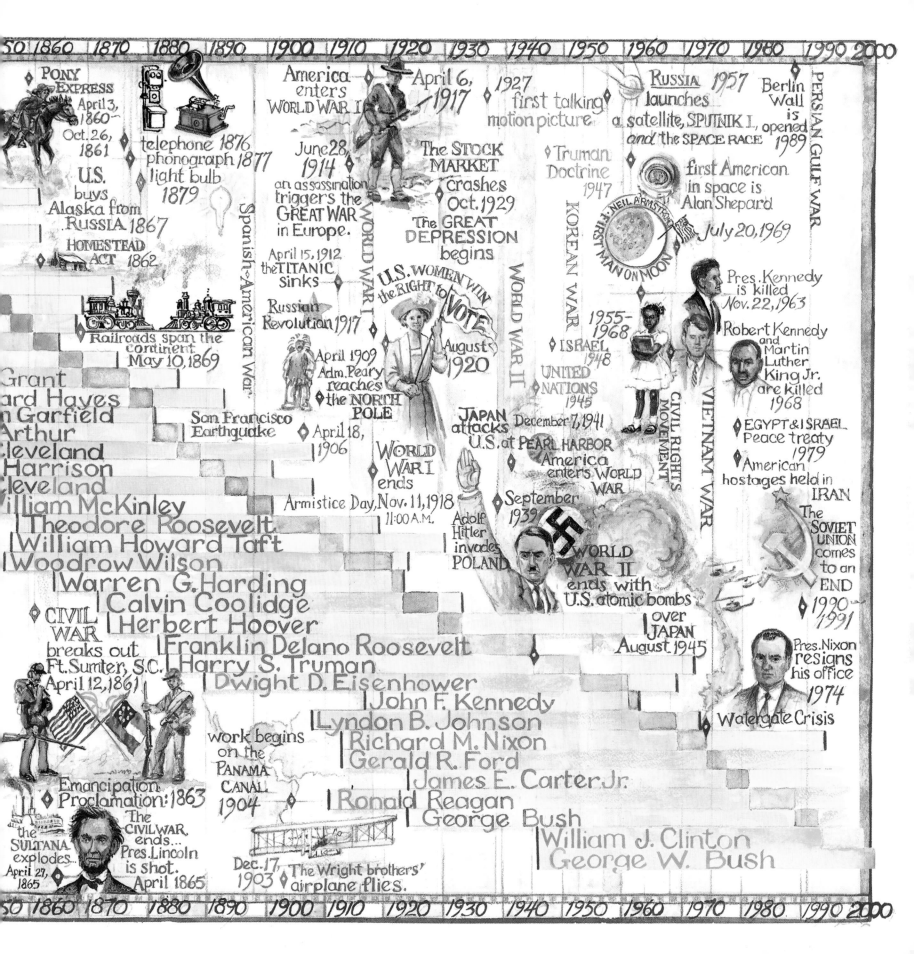

PONY EXPRESS
April 3, 1860 – Oct. 26, 1861

telephone 1876
phonograph 1877
light bulb 1879

U.S. buys Alaska from RUSSIA 1867

HOMESTEAD ACT 1862

Railroads span the continent. May 10, 1869

America enters WORLD WAR I

April 6, 1917

1927 first talking motion picture

Russia 1957 launches a satellite, SPUTNIK I, and 'the SPACE RACE

Berlin Wall is opened 1989

PERSIAN GULF WAR

June 28, 1914 an assassination triggers the GREAT WAR in Europe.

April 15, 1912 the TITANIC sinks

Russian Revolution 1917

Spanish-American War

The STOCK MARKET crashes Oct. 1929

The GREAT DEPRESSION begins

Truman Doctrine 1947

NEIL ARMSTRONG FIRST MAN ON MOON

first American in space is Alan Shepard

July 20, 1969

Pres. Kennedy is killed Nov. 22, 1963

April 1909 Adm. Peary reaches the NORTH POLE

San Francisco Earthquake

April 18, 1906

U.S. WOMEN WIN the RIGHT to VOTE

August 1920

WORLD WAR I

WORLD WAR II

KOREAN WAR

1955–1968

ISRAEL 1948

UNITED NATIONS 1945

CIVIL RIGHTS MOVEMENT

VIETNAM WAR

Robert Kennedy and Martin Luther King Jr. are killed 1968

EGYPT & ISRAEL Peace treaty 1979

American hostages held in IRAN

WORLD WAR I ends Armistice Day, Nov. 11, 1918 11:00 A.M.

JAPAN attacks U.S. at PEARL HARBOR December 7, 1941 America enters WORLD WAR

September 1939 Adolf Hitler invades POLAND

WORLD WAR II ends with U.S. atomic bombs over JAPAN August 1945

The SOVIET UNION comes to an END 1990–1991

Grant
ard Hayes
n Garfield
Arthur
Cleveland
Harrison
Cleveland
illiam McKinley
Theodore Roosevelt
William Howard Taft
Woodrow Wilson
Warren G. Harding
Calvin Coolidge
Herbert Hoover
Franklin Delano Roosevelt
Harry S. Truman
Dwight D. Eisenhower
John F. Kennedy
Lyndon B. Johnson
Richard M. Nixon
Gerald R. Ford
James E. Carter Jr.
Ronald Reagan
George Bush
William J. Clinton
George W. Bush

CIVIL WAR breaks out Ft. Sumter, S.C. April 12, 1861

Emancipation Proclamation: 1863

work begins on the PANAMA CANAL 1904

The CIVIL WAR ends... Pres. Lincoln is shot. April 1865

the SULTANA explodes... April 27, 1865

Dec. 17, 1903 The Wright brothers' airplane flies.

Pres. Nixon resigns his office 1974

Watergate Crisis

Others who have lived in this old house ~

GERALD FORD

born: July 14, 1913
38TH PRESIDENT 1974–77

Congressman Gerald Ford never expected to be president. Nixon's vice president, Mr. Agnew, had resigned, so the president asked Mr. Ford to step in. Then, because of the Watergate scandal, President Nixon resigned his office, too. The unelected vice president took his place and did his best to bring back honesty and dignity to the highest office in the land.

BILL CLINTON

born: Aug. 19, 1946
42ND PRESIDENT 1993—2001

The Arkansas governor was a tireless campaigner in the 1992 race against President George Bush and billionaire Ross Perot. The administration of this energetic young president, the first one born after World War II, was shadowed by uncertainty about America's role as a world power. It was hampered by dissent between Democrats and Republicans in the Congress and the President's own personal and legal misconduct resulting in his impeachment trial in the Senate.

RONALD REAGAN

born: Feb. 6, 1911
40TH PRESIDENT 1981–89

This former movie actor and governor of California had a clear and genial way of communicating his conservative beliefs. President Reagan reduced taxes and enlarged the military during his terms in office. At the same time, the government's debts grew larger. Reagan remained popular throughout his presidency.

JIMMY CARTER

born: Oct. 1, 1924
39TH PRESIDENT 1977–81

A thoughtful man who had been a Naval engineer, a farmer, and governor of Georgia, was elected to the White House in 1976. A champion for human rights, President Carter helped make peace between Egypt and Israel, but he had trouble with Congress, the economy, and terrorists who held 52 Americans hostage for many months in the U.S. Embassy in Iran.

GEORGE W. BUSH

born: July 6, 1946
43RD PRESIDENT 2001

November 7, 2000. For the first time since John Quincy Adams, the son of a president had been elected to the Oval Office. Or had he? Only after five weeks of legal actions and vote recounting was it determined that the cheerful Texas governor had won the long, costly campaign. Bush thus became only the third president in history—and the first in more than a century—to win the White House with a majority of the electoral vote, but a minority of the popular vote.

GEORGE BUSH

born: June 12, 1924
41ST PRESIDENT 1989–93

Two hundred years after George Washington was elected, another George became president. Mr. Bush could have just been a Texas oil millionaire, but he decided to serve his country in Washington, the United Nations, and China. President Bush brought together armies of different nations in a war against Saddam Hussein of Iraq. During his time in the White House, the Soviet Union fell apart and the wall dividing Germany came down, but Americans became less confident about their economy.

1. GEORGE WASHINGTON
2. JOHN ADAMS
3. THOMAS JEFFERSON
4. JAMES MADISON
5. JAMES MONROE
6. JOHN QUINCY ADAMS
7. ANDREW JACKSON
8. MARTIN VAN BUREN
9. WM. HENRY HARRISON

10. JOHN TYLER
11. JAMES POLK
12. ZACHARY TAYLOR
13. MILLARD FILLMORE
14. FRANKLIN PIERCE
15. JAMES BUCHANAN
16. ABRAHAM LINCOLN
17. ANDREW JOHNSON
18. ULYSSES S. GRANT

19. RUTHERFORD B. HAYES
20. JAMES A. GARFIELD
21. CHESTER A. ARTHUR
22/24. GROVER CLEVELAND
23. BENJAMIN HARRISON
25. WM. MCKINLEY
26. THEODORE ROOSEVELT
27. WM. HOWARD TAFT
28. WOODROW WILSON

29. WARREN G. HARDING
30. CALVIN COOLIDGE
31. HERBERT HOOVER
32. FRANKLIN D. ROOSEVELT
33. HARRY S. TRUMAN
34. DWIGHT D. EISENHOWER
35. JOHN F. KENNEDY
36. LYNDON B. JOHNSON
37. RICHARD NIXON

Bibliography

BLASSINGAME, WYATT. *The Look-It-Up Book of Presidents.* New York: Random House, 1993.

BUCKLAND, GAIL. *The White House In Miniature.* New York: W. W. Norton and Company, 1994.

BUTTERFIELD, ROGER. *The American Past.* New York: Simon & Schuster, 1947.

CAROLI, BETTY BOYD. *Inside the White House.* New York: Canopy Books, 1992.

SEALE, WILLIAM. *The President's House: A History.* Washington, DC: White House Historical Association, 1986.

The White House: An Historic Guide. Washington, DC: White House Historical Association, 1962.